I0473889

Marketing Strategies for Self-Published Books

Everything you need to know about local, online and nationwide marketing strategies as well as self-employment taxes.

By

Elisabet Holm

Table of Contents

1. WHERE TO PUBLISH YOUR BOOK.   5

1.1 Recommended Self-Publishing Companies   6

1.2 Self-Publishing Companies to Avoid   15

2. ONLINE MARKETING   20

2.1 Goodreads   21

2.2 Facebook and Twitter   23

2.3 Google   24

2.4 Yahoo   25

2.5 Press Releases   26

2.6 Book Reviews   31

2.7 Blogs and Forums   35

2.8 Your Own Website   36

2.9 Articles   37

2.10 Amazon   38

3. LOCAL MARKETING   40

3.1 Newspapers and radio   41

3.2 Fairs   43

3.3 Bulletin boards   44

3.4 Coffee Shops   45

3.5 Other Places   45

3.6 Book Signings   46

3.7 Volunteering and Donations   47

3.8 Word About Marketing Material   48

4. NATIONWIDE MARKETING   51

4.1 Trade shows   51

4.2 Newspapers and Magazines   54

5. WORD ABOUT TAX DEDUCTIONS   56

5.1 Self-Employment Income and Deductions   56

5.2 Mileage and Business Travel   58

5.3 Entertainment   59

5.4 Business License   60

5.5 Conclusion   61

APPENDIX I   63

APPENDIX II   64

1. Where to Publish Your Book.

Although this book is about marketing and promoting of your self-published book, the first section is dedicated for comparing popular self-publishers. You can find dozens, if not even hundreds of self-publishers or vanity presses that allow you to publish your book as a paperback, hardcover and as an ebook. However, before you spend any time or money in publishing your book, you should know your options, especially which companies to avoid.

If you published your book through a vanity press that charged you hundreds of dollars and pays small royalties, it is not too late to switch your book to a more profitable publisher. Many of the marketing solutions mentioned in this book require you to have a paperback version of your book. If you have only published your book as an ebook, you might want to consider also publishing a paperback. There are a few free to low-cost publishers that print paperbacks, and you should definitely spend the required couple of hours to format your book for this. Not only will you have an actual solid copy to show, but it will also offer an option for those readers that prefer to read a real book.

1.1 Recommended Self-Publishing Companies

Createspace (www.createspace.com).

Createspace is an on-demand or print-on-demand (POD) publishing company that is a part of the Amazon Group of companies. Createspace allows you to publish your book as a paperback for free. You can use their free interior layout tools, free word-file for easy formatting, free cover design and free ISBN service to get your book published within 24 to 48 hours. Createspace pays royalties for every book sold. You do not have to pay a dime to get your book published. Createspace will take their share for every book sold. You can also order your book for a discounted price (a 244 page novel for $3.77 plus shipping, as of March 2012).

Packages: Createspace also offers editing, design and marketing packages starting at few hundred dollars. Examples of their additional services include professional copy-editing for $120, unique book cover for $349 and press-release service for $598.

Distribution. Createspace distributes your books automatically and free through their own online bookstore and Amazon. Optionally you can get your book distributed through Ingram, Baker & Taylor and Lightning Source for a merely $25 onetime fee. Ingram Book Company is the largest book wholesale distributor in the world and the preferred wholesale provider to retail stores such as B&N, independent bookstores and libraries. Baker & Taylor is the second-largest U.S. book wholesaler and also distributes to libraries, bookstores and other institutions worldwide. If you want your book to be available for bookstores you need to enroll for the expanded distribution.

Selling Your Book. Your book will be available within 24 to 48 hours on Amazon and the Createspace store. You will earn a royalty for every book sold. The royalty depends on the manufacturing costs (page number, book size, etc.) and the retailer that sells it. Your royalty can be as high as 80 percent. You can also purchase your own book for a discounted price and sell it personally on your website or hometown.

Royalties: Pays royalties every month. Royalties vary from 10 to 80 percent. Lowest royalties are paid for books sold through the wholesale retailers and highest for books sold through the Createspace store.

Return Policy. Createspace has no-return policy for their books. Meaning that many bookstores will opt out of stocking their shelves with your book, no matter how popular it is, since they cannot return the no-sales. Createspace offers only a 40 percent discount for wholesalers instead of the industry standard 55 percent. This can leave even a very popular book out of bookstore shelves. However, bookstores can still purchase your book if a customer asks to buy one or purchases one through their online site.

Bottom Line: Createspace is easy to use, fast and inexpensive option for a self-publisher. You will get your book published free and for $25 you get it distributed worldwide. You can also issue coupon codes for your book. This is a good way to promote your book. If this your first book, I highly recommend you use Createspace to learn all the aspects of formatting and cover design, before trying another POD such as Lightning Source.

Lighting Source (www.lightningsource.com).

Lightning source is another print-on-demand company. However, unlike Createspace, they do not offer any free tools for creating your book, meaning that you need to have your book formatted and ready for publishing, including designing your own cover. You will simply upload these files to Lighting Source which will then but the book together and print it. You need to pay a one-time set up fee of $37.50 for uploading cover files and $37.50 for uploading interior files.

Account set-up. Setting up an account on Lightning Source can be a hassle. First you need to create a publishing company, which you should do anyways for tax purposes (learn everything you need to know about self-employment taxes and deductions in my book. Once you apply for an account, you need to be approved, which can take few days to weeks.

Distribution. Lighting Source distributes through Ingram, Baker & Taylor, Amazon, B&N and others. You get all this for $12 annual fee per title.

Selling Your Book. You will earn royalties for every book sold through the distribution partners. Lightning Source does not have their own online store to sell books; they just make it available for other retailers. You can also purchase your own book for a discounted price.

Royalties: Pays within 90 days from report date. There is a minimum check writing balance of $25.

Return Policy. Lightning Source allows you to set your own return policy and wholesale discount. If you choose to accept returns and set the industry standard discount of 55 percent, bookstores are more enthusiastic of stocking your book on their selves, since they have the option to return any unsold copies.

Bottom Line: Slightly more expensive than Createspace - both to set your book for sale and to order personal copies. They also charge $30 for a proof copy of your book. If you need to make any changes to your interior or cover files after proof read, you need to pay the fees again. You cannot print a book that already has been printed through another company using the same ISBN. On the positive side—their return policy and wholesale discount is more attractive to bookstores. If you have a print-ready package, meaning you have your book formatted and cover ready, and you believe it could interest a wide array of readers, Lightning Source is a company to consider.

Lulu (www.lulu.com).

Lulu is the second no-fee POD option for printing/publishing your book. There are no fees to make your book available through their online store. You can make paperback, hardcover or even an ebook. You can download a free word-file for easy formatting of your book. They do not offer free cover design. However, they provide easy to follow measurements for creating your cover. You can upload your cover as a PDF file and they provide a preview tool to see that your measurements are correct. The free publishing service does not offer a free ISBN.

Distribution. Lulu distributes through their online store and, if you get a Lulu ISBN for $99.98, they will also make the book available through Amazon. Optionally you can purchase Lulu's distribution package for $75, which makes your book available through Amazon, Baker & Taylor, and B&N. You can either use your own ISBN or purchase an ISBN from Lulu to use this service.

Royalties. You will earn royalties for every book sold. The royalty is considerably less than Createspace offers. You can also purchase your own book for a discounted price. Lulu pays royalties every month.

Packages. You have the option to purchase marketing and publicity packages starting at $4,760. Lulu also offers presentation at trade shows for $195 per show.

Bottom Line: More expensive than Createspace. You need to purchase a Lulu ISBN in order to get your book available through Amazon, when you can get this free through Createspace. You pay another $75 to get it available for bookstores and libraries, compared to $25 through Createspace.

Kindle Direct Publishing (http://kdp.amazon.com)

Kindle is a free ebook publisher. It is a part of the Amazon Group and was the first ebook publisher and distributor. Although many other companies have emerged since, Kindle/Amazon still sells the majority of ebooks. If your ebook is not available through the Amazon Kindle Store, you will miss out a lot of sales.

Book Formatting. Book formatting is a big part of making your ebook look professional; follow the formatting guidelines carefully. You can upload your ebook as a pdf file.

Distribution. Distributes through Amazon.com worldwide. Kindle books can be read on Kindle devices and Kindle apps for iPad, iPhone, iPod touch, Mac, PC, Blackberry, and Android-based devices. You can easily follow your sales through your Kindle Direct Publishing account.

Royalties. Your royalty rate is based on your ebook price. For books listed below $2.98 or above $10, you earn 35 percent of the price. For books priced between $2.99 and $9.99 you will earn 70 percent minus a file deliver cost (usually few cents). Royalties are paid within 60 days after the end of each month.

Bottom Line: Fairly simple to use and pays high royalties for books priced between $2.99 and $9.99. Largest ebook seller in the world.

Smashwords (www.smashwords.com).

Smashwords is another global ebook distributor and one of the only distributors that make your book available through the

Apple iBookstore. Smashwords distributes over 100,000 books from over 35,000 authors worldwide. Smashwords also allows you to issue coupon codes to offer discount for your ebook.

Book Formatting. Smashwords is extremely strict with ebook formatting, mostly because they need to follow the formatting guidelines of all their retail partners. Their ebook formatting guide (www.smashwords.com/books/view/52) is 72 pages long and very frustrating to read. However, if you do not follow the guide and have any formatting errors in your file, your ebook will not be uploaded. Instead you will receive an error message informing what errors were found and how you need to fix them. If you are familiar with word you are fine. For those not so familiar, the formatting might give you a headache. The guide does go over every formatting step and gives pretty detailed instructions how to format your ebook.

Distribution. Smashwords distributes to Apple, Sony, Barnes & Noble, Baker & Taylor, Kobo and Diesel. Your ebook will also be listed at the Smashwords online store. You can easily follow your sales through your Smashwords dashboard.

Royalties. You'll earn 85 percent of the net sales of ebooks sold at the Smashwords.com store and 60 percent of the list price for sales though the distribution network of retailers. Pays quarterly and minimum payment is $10 if paid through Paypal and $75 if paid by check.

Bottom Line: A wide distribution network and good royalty rates. For best distribution of your ebook, make it available through Amazon / Kindle and Smashwords.

Barnes & Noble PubIt

Barnes & Noble released its own ebook reader, Nook, to compete with Amazon's Kindle. Although you can make your ebook available on B&N through Smashwords, you can also upload it directly to the B&N ebook store, PubIt. One reason to do this is to earn 65 percent of your ebook sales, instead of the 60 percent that Smashwords pays.

Book Formatting. Book formatting couldn't be easier than it is with PubIt; you can upload your ebook as a .doc, RTF, HTML or ePub format. View your ebook on the NOOK emulator and fix any errors before publishing.

Distribution. Your ebook will be listed on the B&N online store.

Royalties. You'll earn 65 percent of the ebook price. Pays 60 days after the end of the month. Minimum account balance for payment is $10.

Bottom Line: If you want to earn the extra 5 percent it is worth it.

14

1.2 Self-Publishing Companies to Avoid

Author House (www.authorhouse.com).

Publishing packages start at $749 for hardcover and paperback and $349 for ebooks. Marketing oriented packages start at $4,249 and include business cards, fliers, and posters for you to distribute, and a press-release and an email campaign. Packages include some free copies of your book. Additional copies cost extra. Distributes your book through their own online store as well as through Ingram and Baker & Taylor. Pays royalties every quarter but only when you reach $25.

Bottom Line: You'll pay hundreds of dollars for the same services you'll get for free through Smashwords, Kindle and Createspace. If you want a more aggressive marketing campaign consider hiring a publicist for a month.

Dog Ear Publishing (www.dogearpublishing.net).

Publishing packages start at $1,099. In addition you pay for every book you order. Pays royalties that vary from 8 to 10 percent. Packages include some free copies of your book. Additional copies cost extra.

Bottom line: You'll pay thousands of dollars for something you could do for free through Kindle, Smashwords and

Createspace. Dog Ear also pays lower royalties.

Dorrance Publishing, (www.dorrancepublishing.com)

Dorrance may first seem like a traditional publisher. You need to submit your manuscript for review and they claim not to publish everything they receive. However, after two weeks you'll receive their evaluation in the mail stating they want to publish your book. The catch is that you need to pay $6,000 to $10,000 to get your book published. With that money you'll receive their services including marketing, promotion, editing, design and distribution through Amazon, B&N, Ingram, Baker & Taylor and Lightning Source.

Bottom Line: You won't make any profit until your book has sold 10,000 to 20,000 copies to make up the money you have paid.

Infinity (www.infinitypublishing.com)

Hardcover publishing packages start at $799, ebook packages from $149 and audiobooks from $599. Packages include some free copies of your book. Additional copies cost extra. Expanded distribution through Ingram and Baker & Taylor costs $199. Pays royalties varying from 15 percent to 50 percent.

Bottom line: Distribution to major book retailers is highly

overpriced when compared to Lulu ($75) and Createspace ($25). You pay hundreds of dollars to publish and get smaller royalties than through Createspace.

iUniverse (www.iuniverse.com)

Publication packages at from $899. Packages include some free copies of your book. Additional copies cost extra. All packages include distribution through their online store as well as Ingram and Baker & Taylor. Their most expensive package - $4,449 – also includes some marketing. Pays 20 percent royalty. Pays every quarter, with a minimum balance of $25.

Bottom Line: You pay hundreds to thousands of dollars to get the same services that Createspace offers for $25. Also pays smaller royalties than Createspace.

Outskirtspress (www.outskirtspress.com)

Publication packages start at $199 for black&white. Packages include some free copies of your book. Additional copies cost extra. Also offer ebook publishing services that start from $199. Some packages include marketing and distribution services. Pays royalties that vary depending which publication package and pricing plan you choose. Notice – they claim they pay 100 percent royalties but this means after the wholesale discount, manufacturing and distribution fees are deducted. So do not expect to receive a $25 royalty for a book that you priced at $25. In reality, your royalty (for example for a 200-page, 6"x9" paperback) is between $0.22 to $7.45 and 0.9 to 30 percent (with Createspace you will earn between $6.75 and $16.75 for the same book).

Bottom line: You will pay hundreds of dollars for something you can get for free through Smashwords or Createspace. Your also need to price your book very high to make any money.

Trafford Publishing (www.trafford.com)

Publication packages start at $549 and include ISBN and worldwide distribution. Packages with publicity and marketing start at $3,249. Packages include some free copies of your book. Additional copies cost extra. Pays 20 percent royalty quarterly.

Bottom Line: You pay hundreds to thousands of dollars to get the same services that Createspace offers for $25. Also pays smaller royalties than Createspace.

Xlibris, (www.xlibris.com)

Publication packages start at $499 for paperback and $499 for ebook. Packages with marketing (business cards, press-releases and website design) start at $3,549. Packages include some free copies of your book. Additional copies cost extra. Distributes through their own online store and Ingram. If you want to set the price for your book it will cost extra $249. Pays 25 percent royalty on books sold through their online store and 10 percent on books sold through other retailers. Pays quarterly.

Bottom Line: You pay hundreds to thousands of dollars to get the same services that Createspace offers for $25. Also pays smaller royalties than Createspace.

Xulon Press (www.xulonpress.com)

Publication packages start at $999 and include ISBN and professional marketing specialist services. Distribution costs extra (included on the more costly packages). Royalties vary based on the book price and manufacturing costs – average between 10 and 40 percent.

Bottom Line: You pay hundreds to thousands of dollars to get the same services that Createspace offers for $25. Also pays smaller royalties than Createspace.

2. Online Marketing

Now that you have published your book and are labeled as an indie author, the next step is to promote your book and make it known to your target audience. If you thought publishing your book is all you need to do to sell your book, you were wrong. Publishing merely makes your book available for possible readers, but unless you market your work and make it know, it is very unlikely a reader will accidentally bump into it amongst the hundreds of books that are published every week. As an unknown author, you should concentrate your marketing efforts to both local and online venues.

Online marketing should be one of the cornerstones of your book selling campaign. The options are nearly unlimited when it comes to promoting you and your book in the World Wide Web. Basically you can divide online marketing to two options; those that are free and those that cost. As a self-published or a first time author, the free marketing options obviously sound the most tempting and you may even feel reluctant in spending any money to advertising. After all you have invested all that time and energy on writing your book and now spending money to actually try to sell it doesn't sound fair. However, there are several cost effective online marketing solutions you should definitely consider investing a little bit of time and money. When you know the right venues to place your online advertising, you can have a successful campaign with only cents a day. I will go over some popular websites you should consider. Besides these, you should look into some local websites that might draw your local audience, such as newspapers and other local communities. However, I will talk about these on section 3.

2.1 Goodreads

Goodreads (www.goodreads.com) is an excellent website that helps unite indie authors with readers. The first thing you should do is to join the author program. Joining is free and gives you a profile that allows you to promote yourself and your book to target audience. With the free author program you can also, and should, list your book for a giveaway and lead a Q&A discussion group. The giveaway is an excellent way to obtain free advertisement on the Goodreads website. Your book will be listed on the giveaway page for readers to see. This allows your book to be listed as one of hundreds and not one of thousands. Readers can also add your book to their to-read-list, which is great since you are actually able to see how many readers have done so, giving you an idea how interested people are reading your book. You control what is the start and stop time (days, weeks, months) for the giveaway and how many books you will donate. You need to give a paperback to the winner, an ebook is not acceptable. Once the giveaway ends you will receive an email informing who the winner is and where to send your book. I recommend you save some time and money and have Createspace send the book directly to the winner (you'll pay only one shipping that way). Learn more about the Goodreads author program by visiting www.goodreads.com/author/program.

Besides doing the free author program, you should also set up an advertisement campaign with Goodreads. You can do so with only $10. The Goodreads ad campaign is in many ways superior to Google and Facebook ad campaigns. You will get your ad appear on a website that is visited by millions of book readers. In addition, you get a daily report of your campaign that will tell you how many clicks it received, the number of times your ad was shown per day and how many readers added your book to their to-read-list. Remember, you will only pay when someone actually clicks the ad, not when someone views it or adds it.

2.2 Facebook and Twitter

Having your author page and fan page on Facebook and/or Twitter is a must. These social networking sites are visited by millions of people around the world and, they are one of the most popular ways people, businesses, and products find one another. Keep your author page these separate from your regular Facebook page, but invite all your friends and acquaintances to follow you.

23

You can also advertise on Facebook. However, this can be quite expensive – whatever you set as your daily cap you will reach it (minimum dollar a day). Also the reporting is quite elementary – you don't get as detailed report on the number of clicks and impressions as you do with Google and Goodreads. If you want to try the Facebook campaign, start with a small investment and do not run other online campaigns at the same time. This is to see whether your Facebook campaign is increasing your sales.

2.3 Google

Google AdWords (www.google.com/ads/adwords2/) is another popular place to advertise and probably more worth the money than Facebook. Google ads appear on millions of websites and are targeted on sites or Google searches that use your tag words (explained next). When setting a Google campaign you can set the daily cap and, unlike Facebook, you probably won't reach this cap every day. You'll get a very detailed report on how many clicks your ad received and even which tag words were most successful. Tag words are words that your readers might use when searching anything on Google. If you wrote a book about weight loss your tag words would be something like "weight loss", "losing weight", "lose weight", "diet", "diet that works", etc. When people type these search words, your ad might pop up. Learn more about how to set up a Google campaign and how it works by visiting AdWords Help page (https://support.google.com/adwords/?hl=en).

2.4 Yahoo

Yahoo answers (http://answers.yahoo.com/) is an excellent place to mention your book. This is a place where people can ask anything about anything. The good thing about this site is that most often these questions pop up high in Google search results, drawing lot of readers to the answers. To utilize Yahoo answers, browse for open questions that have something to do with your book and answer them. For example, if you wrote a book about weight loss and someone is asking how to lose weight or what is a good weight loss book, write an answer introducing your book and why it is worth the buy. Do not give specific details. The idea is to give enough details so the person who asks the question or anyone who reads the answers, will become interested in purchasing your book. You might even offer a coupon code for a discount (you can assign coupon codes for books published with Createspace and Smashwords).

2.5 Press Releases

Press release is a good way to announce your book release and should be included to all book publicity campaigns. Press release is a short "news" story that is distributed to the World Wide Web through press release sites. You can send free press releases easily through several sites, including PRLog (www.prlog.org), iNewsWire (www.i-newswire.com/), Free Press Release (www.free-press-release.com), PR.com (www.pr.com), and Your Story (http://your-story.org). These services also offer paid press release submissions. The difference between free and paid press release is mainly distribution. The paid press releases have wider distribution, such as Google news, Yahoo news, and other news services that are subscribed by consumers, journalists and bloggers. However, this does not mean your free press release wouldn't appear on the first page of Google search. You can also add images, and live links to paid press releases.

The best way to take advance of free press releases is to submit one every day or several during a week using more than one press release site. Do at least a month long campaign before and after you release your book. Additionally do special promotions every now and then, introducing lower price or coupon codes in your press releases.

Writing a press release has its own rules. Many of the free press release services won't submit your press release unless it fits their submission guidelines. Press release is always written in third person.

Press Release Guidelines:

1. Headline:

The headline should state your news with a single sentence that captures the attention of your targeted readers. The purpose is to get the reader read the whole press release. Be concise and keep it simple. The headline should be written in title case, meaning every word is capitalized.

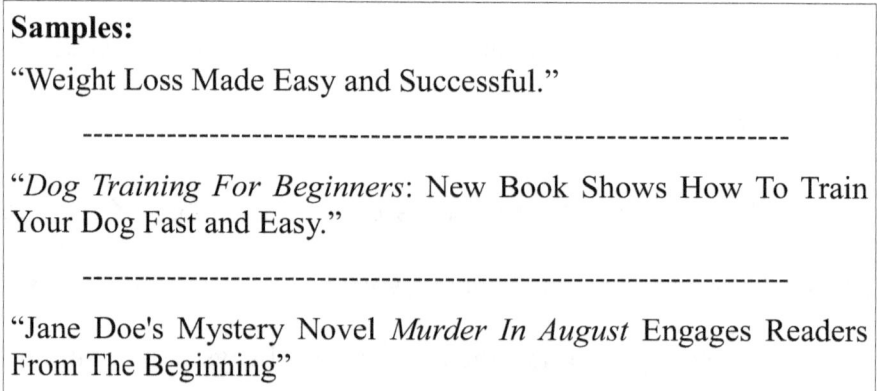

Samples:
"Weight Loss Made Easy and Successful."

"*Dog Training For Beginners*: New Book Shows How To Train Your Dog Fast and Easy."

"Jane Doe's Mystery Novel *Murder In August* Engages Readers From The Beginning"

2. Subhead:

Next you will need to write a two to three sentence subhead

that gives more information for those who decided to read past the headline. The purpose of the subhead is to raise the reader's interest even more in order to have them read the entire press release.

Samples:

"Jane Smith's *Weight Loss Made Easy* promises to make you drop your size in six weeks. For a limited time, get *Weight Loss Made Easy* for $9.99."

"Training your puppy has never been easier than with the detailed instructions of Mark Smith. *Dog Training For Beginners* shows you how to train your dog like a professional."

"Follow private detective John Doe as he hunts a killer through the streets of San Francisco. Jane Doe's Murder in August is already been praised by its readers."

---

3. Body.

Start the body of your press release with City and State. The date is typically added automatically by the press release service.

Divide your press release to three to four paragraphs the following way.

1.   The first paragraph should answer what, where, when, who and why question. If you have a book signing coming, it can introduce the place and time for that. For example you can introduce you and your book.

> Sample:
>
> "Dallas, TX – [date] – Dallas resident Jane Smith releases her new novel *Weight Loss Made Easy* this week. This new weight loss book shows how to make weight loss easy and successful with small changes to your diet and lifestyle."

2.   The second paragraph can expand the first paragraph by providing more info on the book. For example introduce the author and what qualifications he/she has to write the book, write more details about the book, why is the book different from already published books, short author interview or mention any positive

reviews.

3. The third paragraph should mention where to buy the book (with full links so the reader can find the book easily), the price, and a mention of any discounts or coupon codes. If you have a book signing or other event coming, you should also mention that.

4. The fourth paragraph should have an author bio unless you already gave it. Mention any other books you might have published or any on the way. It can also have contact details (website, Facebook, email).

For more samples of press releases visit the following links:

www.webwire.com/FormatGuidelines.asp
www.mediacollege.com/journalism/press-release/format.html

2.6 Book Reviews

Book reviews are a must when promoting your book. Many

people buy a book based on reviews and suggestions by reputable book reviewers or book review sites. Getting your book posted on these sites is a big promotion. Although some book review sites charge to write and post a review, there are dozens of book bloggers and reviewers that write and post book reviews for free (or for a free copy of your book that is). Most of these bloggers will post the review on their own blog as well as popular web sites, such as Indie Book Reviewer, Amazon.com, Smashwords.com and Goodreads.com. The first step in getting your book reviewed is to go through the reviewer listing and find reviewers that accept books in your book genre. Visit every blog/website and find out their submission guidelines. Contact as many reviewers as you can **individually**. Do not send a massive group email to all the reviewers at once. Instead address the reviewer by name, briefly introduce you and your book and give all the important book details (shown below). End your email with a brief ending such as "Thank you for considering [book name]. Hope to hear from you soon.

Details that should be included in every submission:

Book Title:

Author:

Genre:

Word count:

ISBN: (paperback and/or ebook)

Where available:

Back cover description:

Formats you can submit to the reviewer: (paperback or ebook and which ebook formats:.epub, .mobi, PDF, or .doc).

Find contact information for hundreds of book reviewers using the links located below. Remember that these reviewers are busy and sometimes cannot review your book for months or are temporarily closed for review requests. If this is the case, suggest that you can do an author interview and book giveaway. Reviewers love this, especially free copies of your book (paperback or ebook) for their giveaways. Benefits for you are that you get your book posted on their site with dozens if not even hundreds of readers to see it.

Free Indie Book Reviewers

Indie Book Reviewer: http://indiebookreviewer.wordpress.com/

Several indie reviewers post on this site. Review both fiction and non-fiction. Choose the book genre your book belongs to and click on the individual book reviews to get contact information for the different reviewers.

Indie Reader: http://indiereader.com/author-promotional-opportunities/. Online magazine for Indie Books. They do book reviews.

The Indie View: Website that lists indie authors and book reviews. You need to register to gain access to the vast reviewer list.

www.theindieview.com/?checkemail=registered&instance=1.

The Indie Book Podcast: Reviews indie books.

www.indiebookpodcast.com/submissions/

The Indie Book Blog:

http://indiebookblogger.blogspot.com/p/review-sign-up.html

Honest Indie Book Reviews:

34

http://honestindiebookreviews.wordpress.com/

Step-by-Step Self-Publishing: Huge reviewer list.
www.stepbystepselfpublishing.net/reviewer-list.html

Reviewers that Charge

Kirkus Indie: www.kirkusreviews.com/author-services/
BookReview.com: www.bookreview.com/listing.htm

2.7 Blogs and Forums

Join author forums or forums related to the topic of your book. Post comments to these forums mentioning your book. Do not over sell yourself. Be honest and concise. Offer a discount coupon to warm your readers toward buying the book. A good forum for authors is WritersNet (www.writers.net/forum/). It is a good forum to join just to obtain information about publishing and writing in general. If your book is something authors might be interested you can subtly promote it. These are all authors, so do not push it. To find other forums, dedicated for your book genre (etc about weight loss, fiction etc) use Google.

Some popular blogging sites reach hundreds if not even thousands of people every week. Post comments on blogs that are related to your book. You can even ask if the blogger is interested in doing an author interview or a book review. This is something you should ask the book reviewers even if they cannot review your book. It never hurts to ask.

2.8 Your Own Website

You should also consider setting up your own web page. You can do this either by buying your own domain or setting up a free web page. Domains start as low as $0.99 per year. You can also add an email or other services to your account if so desired. GoDaddy (www.godaddy.com) is one place to get your own domain. You will get one free page with your domain – called WebSite Tonight / Instant Page. It is simple to set up, even for beginners, and you can add a picture of you or your book cover, short description and link your Facebook, Twitter and Myspace pages easily to the page.

If you prefer to get a free web page consider Wix.com (www.wix.com). You can name your page (would be www.wix.com/the name you pick]) and pick free templates to set up your page. Wix.com is easy to use and offers several easy to use free-templates. You can even make your book available for sale and add a Paypal link so your readers can purchase the book fast and safely using Paypal.

2.9 Articles

Write an article of your book, an author interview or other blog and offer it to blogging sites, news sites, article posting sites and even your local newspapers. Do not be over promotional. Instead be honest when writing why readers should purchase your book – what would they learn/gain from it.

Sites to offer your article

EzineArticles (www.ezinearticles.com)

Articlebase (www.articlebase.com)

Blogging sites related to your book genre

Local Newspapers

Magazines related to your book genre

2.10 Amazon

Amazon reviews and likes are essential to get your book listed higher in the Amazon search results. Ask your friends and family to post reviews and to click the Like-button. Most book reviewers, mentioned in section 2.6, also post their reviews to Amazon.

Another way you can increase your visibility on Amazon is to post reviews about books similar to yours and post a link to your book on the review. This is very easy to do. Find a book that is similar to yours or might attract same audience. Post a review by clicking the "Post Your Own Review" button at the Custom Reviews section. Write your review and mention a similar book—meaning your book—

that you would recommend. Click the "Insert a Product Link" button and search for your book (note your book must be listed on Amazon in order to do this). Click select and your link is automatically added on your review.

3. Local Marketing

Your local community is one of the best places to start promoting your book. Especially if you live in a small town, you should market your book "as a local author." People may be more intrigued to read your book if it is written by their "neighbor" rather than someone from the other side of the country. This is less true, if you reside in a large city such as New York or Chicago, which are full of authors. In addition of considering the place you currently live as your local community, also consider all nearby towns and the place where you were born or lived previously, if applicable. When it comes to locally promoting your book, connections are everything. Contact everyone you know in your town. Contact their friends and make new acquaintances. The best places to start are small independent businesses that might profit themselves by promoting you.

The first step you should take is to consider who your main audience is. It is entirely different to market a non-fiction book about weight loss than it is to market a fictional young adult or adult novel. You need to target your book promotion to places where your target audience is most likely to spend time. If you wrote an adult mystery, you don't place advertisements to high schools, as you wouldn't place an ad to senior center if you wrote a young adult novel.

3.1 Newspapers and radio

Contact all of your local newspapers, whether they are small or large, and inquire if they are interested in doing an author interview or book review. Local newspapers love writing about their local celebrities, even if you do not consider yourself as one. When you contact your local newspaper, do not send a random email to a general email address, unless this is the only one you find. Instead find the name and email (or phone number) of the person who is responsible for community news, arts, book reviews or similar department that would be interested in writing a story about a local author.

In addition to your local commercial newspapers, consider contacting any small publications that are distributed to very specific neighborhoods in your town. If you are unsure about the papers that are distributed in your town and cannot find any by doing a Google search, check newsstands and the entrance / exit of your local grocery store, coffee shop, or restaurant. These often carry free community newspapers.

Radio stations are another source that reaches thousands of listeners. Just as the newspapers, local radio stations are often interested in doing stories about local people. Listen to the different shows aired on each station in order to get an idea who to contact and which radio host would be the best fit on doing a story on you or your book. This information is rarely listed on the website. Whether you contact a newspaper or radio station, offer to send a signed copy of your book to the person interested in doing a story of you.

If you wrote a young adult novel or a non-fiction book that

might interest younger audience, consider contacting local high school newspapers.

3.2 Fairs

Your town most likely has several fairs and events throughout the year. Whether it is craft fairs, farmer's markets, county fairs or similar, these are places where people come together in masses. Thus, these are the places where you can reach a large number of possible readers.

Consider taking a booth on your local craft fair. These are usually very inexpensive and a good place to sell your book combined with book signing. Contact local schools and churches, which are popular places for craft fairs.

Farmer's market is another place where you can meet lots of people possibly interested in your book. Place fliers around the area for the day of the event. Even if fliers are not allowed normally, a busy event like farmer's market is an easy way to sneak them in. Same goes for other, bigger events. Place fliers and bookmarks where you can and remove them after the event is over.

3.3 Bulletin boards

Your town is full of free advertising space in the form of bulletin boards. You can find these on grocery stores, community centers, churches and schools. When combined, you will reach a large part of your community with these boards.

Make an interesting flier (I will talk more about fliers in section 3.6) that promotes your book and place it on these bulletin boards. This sounds easy, but it means a lot of driving and time to actually distribute these fliers around your town. Placing one flier to one store won't do it. Visit as many places you can think of that have a community bulletin board and place your ad. Some places clear their boards every week, so you might want to consider doing a trip once or twice a month to check if you need to replace the flier.

3.4 Coffee Shops

Although you might not see people reading books at coffee shops, it doesn't mean your target audience is not visiting them... every day. Coffee shops are an excellent venue to place bookmarks that will advertise your book (see section 3.8 for marketing material to learn more about bookmarks). Unfortunately Starbucks does not accept promotional material, which is a shame since they are occupying so many street corners. However, you can surely find independent coffee shops from your town where to place free bookmarks for the customers to take.

3.5 Other Places

When it comes to finding places where to market your book, the sky is the limit. There are hundreds of places in your town where you can and should place a flier or a bookmark advertising your book. Think about the target audience for your book and where they would most likely spend time; parks, bus stops, subway stations, community centers, churches, shopping malls, schools, playgrounds, health clubs. Grocery store bulletin boards are obviously one of the best places to reach your target audience since everyone needs to buy food. However, there are other places where you can reach your readers as well. For example, if you wrote fitness, health or beauty related book, go to beauty salons, hair salons, spas, health clubs and health food stores and ask if you can place a flier or bookmarks for the customers to see and take. If you wrote a fictional novel, ask if you can place fliers or bookmarks to bookstores, parks, playgrounds (for moms to see), boutiques, and restaurants. Promotional material for young adult novels should definitely go to high schools, parks, fast food restaurants near schools, yogurt shops, music shops, and clothing stores. Always ask the employees or owner can you place fliers in the premises.

3.6 Book Signings

Bookstores rarely arrange book signings for self-published authors. However, it never hurts to go to your local bookstore in person and ask them. In addition to bookstores, you can arrange a book signing in restaurants—think about a wine tasting and book signing event—coffee shops, libraries, or even a special location that fits your books genre. These would include toy stores if you wrote a children's book, high schools if you wrote a young adult novel, health stores and salons if you wrote a book about health and fitness, or wine stores if you wrote a book about food and wine. Use your imagination and approach your local business owner – they will get customers, you will get publicity.

3.7 Volunteering and Donations

Volunteering and donating your book to a charity raffle or other event is a good way to get publicity. Contact your local churches, environmental agencies, schools, and any other place you can think of that arranges events run by volunteers. Ask if you can place your fliers and/or bookmarks around the event in return for your volunteer action. Many schools and churches organize events that have a raffle. Donate a copy of your book as a price and maybe in return you can hand off fliers or place bookmarks for people to take.

3.8 Word About Marketing Material

Marketing or your book promotion material includes fliers, business cards, bookmarks, and coupon codes. These are essential when marketing your book to your local community. You can order professional fliers through an online print service such as Vistaprint (www.vistaprint.com) or 4imprint (www.4imprint.com), or make your own easily using Microsoft Word or Powerpoint or any image software. To make your marketing material look professional use photo paper instead of regular print paper.

Flier is a 1/3 of a page to one page advertisement about your book. Post fliers onto bulletin boards, parks, coffee shops and anywhere else you can think of. This is an excellent and cheap way to promote your book in your local community. See an example of a flier in Appendix I.

Bookmarks are one of the best ways to promote your book. The front of the bookmark should be appealing picture that makes it desirable for the consumer. The backside of the bookmark should be a short and simple advertisement of your book. Place free bookmarks in a small basket to coffee shops, small boutiques, bookstores and any other place you can think of. Customers of these establishments can take your free bookmark and at the same time get an ad of your book they will carry with them. You can order bookmarks from Overnight Prints (www.overnightprints.com/bookmarks) or Impressive Creations (www.impressiveinscriptions.com/), or make them yourself. See an example of a bookmark in Appendix II.

Business cards are another way you can promote your book. They are not as good as bookmarks, which have a purpose for the consumer. If you do not have the time to make bookmarks, distribute business cards to the same places as bookmarks.

Discount coupon codes are an excellent way to draw the attention of possible readers. Many people find discounts intriguing and can make them purchase your book just for the sake of the discount. If you publish your book through Createspace or Smashwords you can easily assign online coupon codes for your book. Place these codes in your press releases, websites, Facebook, Twitter, fliers, bookmarks or business cards.

4. Nationwide Marketing

4.1 Trade shows

Trade shows are places where book lovers and book professionals get together and learn about new book releases. There are dozens of trade shows around the U.S. annually and getting your book presented in one or more of these is good promotion. Traditional publishers often have a booth on trade shows in order to promote their new releases in their booth and on the trade show catalog. Unfortunately the booths usually cost thousands of dollars, and thus, even if there is a trade show near your town, it is usually not worth the money to get a booth on your own. Luckily there are book promoting companies that sell spots on their booth and catalog. You do not need to be present yourself. You just need to send two copies of your book to the company and they do the rest. One of the best priced ones is Combined Book Exhibit (www.combinedbook.com). They do dozens of fairs every year and you can get your book presented for $195 per show ($129 if you join as a member). They also offer ad space on the trade catalog and other promotional services. If you have the money to do this, and if your book is something that could interest libraries, you should consider doing one or two shows.

You can also advertise or participate directly through the show organizer. Below is a list of book festivals you should consider attending.

The Houston Indie Book Festival (http://indiebookfest.org/)

West Hollywood Book Fair (www.westhollywoodbookfair.org/)

LA Times Festival of Books (http://events.latimes.com/festivalofbooks)

National Book Festival (www.loc.gov/bookfest/)

Southern Festival of Books (www.humanitiestennessee.org/programs/southern-festival-books/about-southern-festival-books)

Central Coast Book and Author Festival (http://slolibraryfoundation.org/CCBAF2.html)

Self-Publishing Book Expo (http://selfpubbookexpo.com/)

Vegas Valley Book Festival (www.artslasvegas.org/vvbf/)

Printers Row Lit Fest (www.chicagotribune.com/entertainment/books/printersrowlitfest/

)

Baltimore Book Festival (www.baltimorebookfestival.com/)

Litquake (http://litquake.org/)

Santa Barbara Book and Author Festival (www.sbbookfestival.org/index.html)

Kentucky Book Fair (http://kybookfair.org/)

Amelia Island Book Festival (http://ameliaislandbookfestival.com/)

The Spring Book Show (www.gabbs.net/GABBS_Atlanta.html)

South Carolina Book Festival (www.scbookfestival.org/)

Wordstock (www.wordstockfestival.com/)

Festival of Reading (www.festivalofreading.com/)

Twin Cities Book Festival (www.raintaxi.com/bookfest/)

Nebraska Book Festival (http://bookfestival.nebraska.gov/2012/index.aspx)

Wisconsin Book Festival (www.wisconsinbookfestival.org/about)

The West Port Book Festival (http://westportbookfestival.org/)

Notice the following book festivals/competitions you should avoid as they might be a scam!

DIY Convention (www.diyconvention.com/)

The Halloween Book Festival (www.halloweenbookfestival.com/)

San Francisco Book Festival (www.sanfranciscobookfestival.com/)

The Hollywood Book Festival (www.hollywoodbookfestival.com/index.html)

The New York Book Festival (www.newyorkbookfestival.com)

The Beach Book Festival (www.newyorkbookfestival.com/)

4.2 Newspapers and Magazines

Getting your book reviewed or advertised in a nationwide newspaper and/or magazines means lot of publicity. Unfortunately this is easier said than done. Most newspapers and magazines that review books, such as New York Times, Washington Post, and Book Reporter, don't usually review self-published books. What to do? Well the World Wide Web is the limit. Contact newspapers and magazines in your state first or, if you wrote a non-fiction, contact magazines that specialize on the topic your book is about. Offer to send a copy of your book if they want to do a review and/or author interview. This can be time consuming and only result few hits but any review or article you can get is free publicity. Other option is to place advertisements on these newspapers or magazines.

5. Word About Tax Deductions

Please note that this information is for informational purposes only. The author waives all responsibility for the information presented in this chapter. Tax laws change every year and you should familiarize yourself with the most current laws or hire a tax professional. Although taxes are not due until April the following year, you need to start collecting receipts for your tax deductions immediately. This means saving every receipt of qualified expenses, track every mile you drive for business purposes, and save every home expense invoice that qualify for an expense. Disclaimer:

5.1 Self-Employment Income and Deductions

The income you make as an independent contractor is considered as self-employment or business income. Technically you have a home-based business if you work from home as a freelance writer. Even if you work outside your home full- or part-time, the income you earn (or lose) as an author needs to be claimed as self-employment income in your taxes.

Fortunately, you can lower your tax bill with qualified deductions, which include all the obvious business expenses, such as a new computer, printer, pencils, paper, advertising, monthly internet fee, monthly phone fee, etc. If you are a member of professional associations, the annual fees are deductible. In other words, any expense you have in relation to your business is tax deductible.

Besides these common office expenses, you can also deduct the mileage you drive for business purposes, such as when distributing your marketing material locally or even long distance (which is considered a business travel and talked more in the next section).

In some cases you can also deduct part of your rent and home expenses. This applies if you "rent" out an office space from your home. There are some rules for doing this though. For example, the space you rent from your home cannot be used for other purposes -

such as your kitchen or bedroom, it has to be used major of the time for your home business.

5.2 Mileage and Business Travel

Anytime you drive your car for business purposes, you can deduct the mileage from your taxes. You must remember that any expense you claim must be documented in case you get audited. This is easy to do for expenses that have receipts. However, for the mileage you drive, there are no receipts (you do not deduct gas expenses). In order to document your mileage – record the day, route and distance you drive, as well as the purpose for each trip. A good way to do this is to use Microsoft Excel or other computer program. As of 2012 one mile equals 55.5 cents. This means that if you drive 1000 miles a year for business purposes, you can deduct $555.

Business travel is another deduction you can make. Traveling to promote your services or participating in conferences can be deducted as an expense. Also meals, accommodation, and air travel tickets can be deducted, if the main purpose of the travel was business related. Business travel includes trips that you take to distribute your marketing material, book signings, author interviews, conferences, and trade fairs. Save all the meal, lodging and travel receipts (no gas receipts needed just the mileage you drive) and record every promotional stop you make (store name, city, and state). You can travel with your family, but you cannot deduct their meals, lodging or air travel expenses.

If you use your car for business purposes, remember to save every receipt that goes to car repair and insurance. These are also deductible.

5.3 Entertainment

Entertainment is another big deduction you can do with certain limits. Entertainment costs include restaurant bills and similar expenses that you can justify to be business related. For example, if you have a business meeting, such as interviewing a source for a book or article, or talking about marketing plans, this qualifies as a business expense. If you have your meeting at a restaurant, you can deduct the meals and drinks. You need to pay the entire bill and show the receipts. In addition, you need to record "why, where, when and with who" aspect of the meeting. Do this by first making a copy of the receipt (since many of them fade over time). Then write down the person(s) involved, the topic of the conversation, where the meeting was held, and when it was held.

Learn more about business entertainment and travel expenses at

http://www.irs.gov/publications/p463/ch02.html#en_US_2012_pub link100033852

5.4 Business License

Whether you need a business license depends on the city and state you live in. Generally business license costs a few hundred dollars a year (which is tax deductible). If you work from home you most likely won't need a city business license, which is meant for businesses that operate outside the home. Some states allow you to file the business license for free if you operate your business from home and your net earnings are no more than 66 2/3 percent of the average annual wages. Find out the regulations of your state by visiting the secretary of state website of your local state.

5.5 Conclusion

Start saving your receipts and marking down you're the mileage you drive. It is better to save every receipt, even those that you are unsure whether they qualify as an expense. When it is time to do your taxes—hire a tax professional, especially if you are unfamiliar with business / self-employment taxes. Remember that you can deduct your tax preparation fees in your next year's taxes, so using a qualified tax professional is cost effective. Also it is important to note that even if your business expenses were more than what you earned during a year, this is considered as a business loss and you can claim that too. For more information about self-employment and business taxes, visit the IRS website (www.irs.gov/businesses/small/article/0,,id=115045,00.html).

Appendix I

Sample Flier

[your headline here with a font size 36 to 40 and in color]

[your subhead here]]   [book cover picture here]

eBook [price]
paperback [price]

[where can your book be purchased here]

[your email/website here]

Appendix II

Sample bookmark.

Make the bookmark 4" by 1.5" or bigger. Print your bookmark, glue the two pieces together and place a satin ribbon between the two papers   to make the bookmark. Use photo paper for the front picture and thick scrapbook paper for the back picture.

Front   BACK

[title of your book] by [your name]
[your headline] novel from [city you live] author.
Available [mention major retailers where available]
eBook [price], Paperback [price].
Get $2 off from paperback when you use coupon code [add your code]
only at www.createspace.com/[your page]

Note: The picture in this bookmark is designed by Elisabet Holm. You are free to use it for your bookmarks.

www.ingramcontent.com/pod-product-compliance
Lightning Source LLC
Chambersburg PA
CBHW071631170526
45166CB00003B/1278